THE DUMBEST CROOK BOOK

Originally published as *The Stupid Crook Book*

Leland Gregory

SCHOLASTIC INC.

New York Toronto London Auckland Sydney
Mexico City New Delhi Hong Kong Buenos Aires

ISBN 0-439-74080-0

12 11 10 9 8 7 6 5 4 3 2 1   5 6 7 8 9 10/0

Printed in the U.S.A.   23

First Scholastic printing, January 2005

Book design by Holly Camerlinck

This book is dedicated to my wife and partner in crime, Gloria Graves Gregory. I love you and I'm honored to be spending my life with you.

Introduction

First let me say that I know that to be grammatically correct this book should be titled *The Book of Dumb Crooks*. But honestly, a book about bumbling burglars, dim-witted robbers, dumb pickpockets, intellectually challenged confidence men, boneheaded bank robbers, and thickheaded thieves doesn't really warrant it; and besides, *The Dumbest Crook Book* is funnier. In most cases I've altered or eliminated the names of the suspects or criminals because, even though in most cases they're extremely stupid, they still have the ability to hire lawyers. In every instance, however, the facts are true and have been taken strictly from legitimate news sources (there are no Siamese-twin criminals who have lost 150 pounds on the alien-Bigfoot diet). I would like to extend my undying gratitude to the men and women of law enforcement who put their lives on the line every day to keep us safe and who are forced to wade into the shallow end of the gene pool when dealing with the type of dummies included in this book.

TWO DUMBELLS

*T*he alarm sounded at the Buffum-Downtown YMCA
in Long Beach, California, and the police arrived
within five minutes. They soon discovered two men trying
to steal six forty-five-pound barbells that were loaded into
a rickety shopping cart. Too bad the two thieves were
two ninety-five-pound weaklings, because the shopping
cart kept tipping over on them as they tried to escape.
"They weren't even very big guys," said Tim Hardy, phys-
ical education director at the gym. When the police cornered them, the two thieves struggled to lift the barbells
into a trash bin. They were quickly arrested and placed
on $5,000 bond each. There was no explanation why the
two dumbbells wanted the six barbells—they were only
worth about sixty cents a pound. Maybe they knew they
would eventually be arrested and wanted to tone up
before going to prison.

SAVE ME FROM MYSELF

*M*ost of the stories in this book show how one, or maybe two, very stupid actions can result in the arrest of a criminal. But one Pittsburgh, Pennsylvania, criminal (whom I'll lovingly refer to as Our Crook) holds the record for moronic moves—eight to be exact. Here they are, in chronological order, a clumsy criminal's attempts to break into a shed, a garage, and a home.

Moronic Move Number One: Our Crook smashes his fist through a window in the shed—shredding his hand.

Moronic Move Number Two: Our Crook successfully breaks into the second story of the nearby garage. The garage is dark; Our Crook doesn't have a flashlight, doesn't see the hole in the floor, falls through it, and winds up bruised, dazed, and confused on the first floor.

Moronic Move Number Three: While staggering around on the first floor of the garage, our bewildered burglar falls into the grease pit—cracking his cranium.

Moronic Move Number Four: The garage has gotten the best of Our Crook, so he decides to break into the house. He shatters the window in the front door, creeps inside, and promptly tumbles down the cellar stairs.

Moronic Move Number Five: Our Crook finally realizes this isn't his day. He leaves the house and gets into his car. He drives downhill, loses control of the car, and hits a tree. His already damaged head (see Moronic Move Number Three) strikes the steering wheel with great force.

Moronic Move Number Six: Not wanting any criminal element to get away with his getaway car, Our Crook gets out of his car and locks all the doors. For some reason he then retraces his steps to the garage and retraces his fall into the grease pit.

Moronic Move Number Seven: Our Crook staggers out of the garage and decides to go back home. He reaches into his pocket to retrieve his car keys but can't find them. He smashes his car's rear window, climbs in over the backseat, and breaks the gearshift getting the car into neutral. As the car begins rolling down the hill, Our Crook pops the clutch to jump-start the car—and he succeeds, but he can't unlock the steering wheel. He crashes into a second tree.

Moronic Move Number Eight: The third blow to his head causes Our Crook to lose consciousness. His noggin falls against the steering wheel, setting off the car horn. The blaring horn alerts the neighbors, who call the cops, who arrest Our Crook. He pleads guilty to a charge of criminal mischief (he never actually stole anything) and is christened the Bad-Luck Burglar by the police.

I don't know about you, but I feel humbled in the presence of such overwhelming stupidity.

A MIND IS A TERRIBLE THING TO READ

You're in the middle of a home robbery. You've just discovered a diamond ring but you're wondering where the other "good" stuff could be hidden. What do you do? Well, one burglar who found himself in such a predicament picked up the phone and dialed a psychic hot line. The thief didn't just have a quick chat with the psychic; he stayed on the line long enough to total $250 in charges. How was our nonclairvoyant criminal apprehended? While chatting away with the psychic, he used his real name. When the phone bill came in later that month, the homeowners saw the outrageous 900-number call and called the police, who traced it back to the psychic. Even though the crook was dumb enough to use his real name, a truly gifted psychic, in my opinion, should have known who he was anyway.

According to the FBI, the average number of bank robbers who are arrested each year because they were stupid enough to write their holdup notes on the backs of their own deposit slips: forty-five.

DELI DOS AND DON'TS

*N*atron Fubble quickly entered a Miami delicatessen and placed his order. Instead of asking for a nice egg-salad sandwich, Fubble asked for all the money in the cash register. And instead of giving him the cold, hard cash, the owner smashed him in the face with a cold, hard salami. Fubble fumbled out of the delicatessen and hid himself and his pulsating proboscis in the trunk of a parked car. Unknown to Fubble, he had chosen as his hideaway the trunk of an undercover police team who were staked out observing another criminal's activities. Police officers finally heard Fubble's moaning and his attempts to breathe through his salami-snapped septum. But they didn't discover him immediately; you see, the officers weren't in the car at the time of Fubble's arrival . . . and didn't return to it for five days. Being locked in a trunk for five days, it's probably a good thing Fubble's nose *was* out of commission.

TRAFFIC JAM

*T*hings were going smoothly for a burglar as he broke into the Hill-Rom Corporation in Pennsauken, New Jersey. He had opened the door and, as he had seen hundreds of times in the movies, knew exactly how to keep the lock from latching behind him. He removed a piece of paper from his pocket, folded it, and carefully placed the paper between the latch and the door frame, ensuring that the door wouldn't lock while he was scampering about inside, cleaning out the place. His deed done, he left through the door he had ingeniously rigged and made his escape. When the police arrived to investigate the robbery, they noticed a folded piece of paper by the doorjamb. They opened it and the case was solved. It wasn't a confession—it was a traffic ticket. The ticket, complete with home address and telephone number, had been issued to the burglar the night before, citing him for driving with a cracked windshield. He was promptly arrested and all the stolen property was recovered. A cracked windshield, huh? Sounds like a pretty good description of the suspect, doesn't it?

In Wellington, New Zealand, a young man held a radio-station manager hostage, locked the both of them in the studio, and forced him to play the song "The Rainbow Connection" by Kermit the Frog.

IT'S DÉJÀ VU ALL OVER AGAIN

*I*f at first you don't succeed, try, try again" must have been running through the mind of this story's repeat offender sometime during his short criminal career. The Troy, Alabama, man was arrested and pleaded guilty to breaking into the Deja Vu store–twice. Our recidivist, who apparently wasn't very original, smashed the same window and stole much of the same merchandise. He was arrested because the same witness identified him both times. I wonder if he'll get off because of the rule of double jeopardy?

A survey published in Whittle Communications' SPECIAL REPORT magazine revealed that 27 percent of home burglars like to raid the refrigerator while on the job.

TAKE A HIKE

The clerk stood terrified as the knife-wielding robber loomed in front of him. He did just as he was asked, turning over everything in the cash register, all of sixty-nine dollars. But the thief wanted more. On his way out he confiscated a pair of tan hiking boots, then hit the getaway trail. The accused robber was apprehended and held over for trial. During the proceedings the clerk positively identified the defendant as the man who perpetrated the robbery—but other than an identification, the prosecuting attorney had little evidence to convict. That's when the defendant started feeling confident about getting released and propped his feet up on the table. "I leaned over and stared," said Judge James Fleetwood. "I said, 'Surely nobody would be so stupid as to wear the boots he stole to his trial.'" The clerk quickly identified the tan hiking boots on the defendant's feet as the ones lifted from his store. The jury barely turned on their heels before they found him guilty of aggravated robbery. He was taken away and his boots were confiscated. "We sent him back to jail in his stocking feet," Fleetwood added. If they always remove stolen items from your person before they send you to jail, it's a good thing the guy hadn't stolen a pair of pants and underwear.

A TURN FOR THE WORSE

A patrolman in Suffield, Connecticut, spotted a speeding car and began pursuit. The officer was informed that the vehicle matched the description of one used in the robbery of a bakery seven miles north of town. The driver looked in the rearview mirror and quickly realized he was being chased. He thought he would outsmart the cops—but you've got to have smarts to do that. He pulled into a spacious parking lot, jumped out of his car, and ran into the front lobby of a large building to hide. He was surprised, however, when the doors closed behind him and locked. "I believe he thought it was a mall," said Patrolman Michael Lewandowski. "But I've never seen too many malls with razor wire across the top." The fast-driving but slow-thinking criminal had pulled into the parking lot of MacDougall Correctional Institution, a high-security prison. He was charged with several motor vehicle offenses and with being a fugitive from justice. And some people claim men are bad with directions—this guy knew where he was headed all along.

A woman in Elgin, Texas, was arrested and charged with shoplifting. The woman was seen taking an item off the shelf, walking around the store devouring the contents, and then leaving without paying for it. She was charged with stealing a jar of pickled pigs' feet.

SPACE CADETS

*W*hat's taking so long?" thought one of the two robbers of a local grocery store in Larch Barrens, Maryland. The dim-witted duo thought the laser they had stolen earlier would cut through the store's safe like it was butter. Maybe they had the setting wrong. Maybe the safe was stronger than they thought. Or maybe they were just stupid. When the police arrived, the two were still hunched over the safe, trying to cut through to the money hidden inside. The police confiscated the laser, and the two admitted they had stolen it from a local amusement center earlier in the day. It was a Lazer Tag gun, a battery-operated toy, and the two had been shining its harmless light on the safe for nearly an hour before the police arrived. Beam me up, Scotty. There's no sign of intelligent life on this planet.

The timing was off for a bank robber in Cheshire, Massachusetts. He pulled off the heist at 4:30 P.M. and tried to make his getaway through downtown North Adams. Stuck in rush-hour traffic, he was apprehended by an officer on foot.

DOG-DAY AFTERNOON

*I*mages of a feast with sirloins and ribs, T-bone steaks, filet mignon, veal, roasts, and other delicacies must have crossed the minds of the thieves when they broke into a commercial freezer and stole nine bundles wrapped in black plastic. As they loaded up their car, they probably discussed what would be good side items: baked potatoes, a garden salad with vinaigrette dressing, Jell-O? Their mouths were watering, and they couldn't wait to get home and fire up the grill. They lost their appetites, I'm sure, when they unwrapped the packages and discovered the frozen bodies of dogs, cats, and a ferret or two. Apparently the crooks didn't notice that the freezer was located behind the Paradise Valley Road Pet Hospital. There could be a new advertising slogan in all this: "Fido, the other white meat!"

THE CALL OF THE WILD

A burglar had quietly broken into a baker's shop in Villach, Austria, completely unaware that he was being watched. He was looking around the shop with a flashlight, trying to locate the safe, when suddenly he was attacked–by Lola the cockatoo. Caught completely off guard, the robber flailed about and accidentally knocked over a glass tank, setting free Egor, a viper. While trying to fight off the enraged cockatoo, who had become entangled in his hair, the robber watched in horror as the snake slowly slithered toward him. Enjoying the whole show from the safety of his cage was Peppino, the shop owner's pet mynah bird. Not wanting to be left out of the action, Peppino blurted out his favorite imitation–that of a doorbell ringing. The burglar decided to make a run for it and ran right through the shop's front window. When the store's owner came down to see what all the commotion was about, he saw his escaped pets and the escape route the burglar had taken. He also noticed blood around the window frame, as well as small pieces of the burglar's clothing left on the glass–the two thousand schillings in his safe, however, had been untouched. I've heard of a smash-and-grab thief before, but not a grab-and-smash.

WELL, HE WAS UNDER OATH

A man convicted of robbery asked the Texas Court of Appeals to overrule his guilty verdict on the basis of a self-incriminating answer given at his trial. During a break in the trial, there was concern that the suspect had fraternized with some witnesses who were to take the stand against him. The judge asked the suspect to tell him exactly which witnesses he had contacted, and the man answered, "The ones that I robbed."

Seventy-five dollars was stolen from a Chicago man by a robber using a manhole cover as a weapon.

A ROBBERY THAT WAS IN THE BAG

To pull off a successful bank robbery you not only need to have a well-thought-out plan, you must also accomplish the listed items on the plan in order. It was the last part in Bank Robbery 101 that this Charlotte, North Carolina, man didn't grasp. He remembered the gun; he remembered the getaway car; he even remembered to wear a disguise. As disguises go, however, it wasn't the most original—a simple paper bag with eyeholes cut out. The problem wasn't with having the mask, it was when he decided to put it over his head—while he was driving the car and still blocks from the bank. Several drivers noticed the "unknown driver" and called police about the suspicious man wearing a bag over his head. The robber pulled up to the bank, got out of his car, and walked straight to a teller to make his demands. The teller had a hard time understanding the bagged bad guy because he had forgotten to cut a mouth hole in the bag. Finally, he made himself understood, got his hands on a fistful of money, and ran out of the bank. Of course by this time the man's plans had been let out of the bag by the numerous calls to the police, and he was arrested immediately after he exited the bank.

CRIMINAL ON DISPLAY

*T*ellers at a branch of the Bank of New Hampshire in Littleton were suspicious of a man they saw loitering in the bank's foyer. He had been there awhile but had made no attempt to enter the bank. What piqued the tellers' attention was the fact that the man was wearing a ski mask. Officers arrived on the scene and questioned the man, who claimed he was wearing the mask because it was cold. It *was* cold outside, so that *could* explain the mask; but what the man couldn't explain was why he was carrying a BB pistol in his pocket and a note reading, "Give me all your money or I'll shoot you."

When a teller in Swansea, Massachusetts, told a would-be bank robber she had no money, he fainted. He was still unconscious when the police arrived. When the police found his getaway car, they discovered that the keys were locked inside it.

ONE SMALL STEP FOR MAN

*L*os Angeles County police were summoned by an emergency call to Ricks Liquor Store on a break-in complaint. Police arrived to find a twenty-three-year-old man alone in the locked store. "When they got there, they could see him sitting on the floor by the front counter, smoking a cigarette and drinking a beer," said Sergeant John O'Neal. "The cigarettes and the lighter were his." The burglar had helped himself to a beer from a case stacked on the floor. The police quickly surmised that the thief had cut a hole in the roof and entered the building through the air ducts. "After a few minutes, he realizes he can't get back out. So what do you think he does? He calls 911," Los Angeles police sergeant Roger Ferguson said. "The 911 operator at first didn't believe him. She thought it was a joke." But the sequestered suspect finally convinced the dispatcher, and she alerted the police. The store's owner was called to open the metal gate and door. He told police that two other burglars in the past two years had used the same method to get in—they couldn't get out either—but this criminal was the first to call the police.

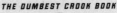

An Egyptian man carjacked a vehicle and drove it several miles before pulling over to the side of the road and leaving with the car's stereo system. The reason the man decided not to steal the car? He was blind.

ON THE CUTTING EDGE

A convicted criminal being escorted to jail in St. Petersburg, Florida, somehow managed to escape and go on the lam. During his escape, however, he suffered several deep cuts to his feet, but even with the loss of blood the criminal was able to vanish into thin air, and the authorities didn't have a clue as to his whereabouts. They got their break from the most unexpected of places—the local hospital. The authorities at the hospital got suspicious of their most recent patient—not because of his wounds but because of his words. When asked to fill out the standard hospital forms, on the line about the cause of the injury our escapee wrote, "Escape from jail."

An attempted robbery of the Household Federal Savings Bank in Reston, Virginia, ended when a teller, after reading the robber's holdup note, reached across the counter and punched the man in the face, sending him racing from the building.

THE LETTER OF THE LAW

The sheriff of Fincastle, Virginia, opened a letter addressed to him and was shocked and horrified at what he read. The letter, with no lack of detail, threatened to torture and kill the sheriff and the members of his family. It was obvious from the return address that the author of the letter was already a resident at the jail, so he was approached about the letter. The convict claimed he meant no harm with the letter but was simply doing research as to whether the sheriff opened his own mail or not. For writing these few sentences, the convict had a few more years added to his sentence.

WHO LET THE DOGS OUT?

*T*wo men in Newark, New Jersey, were arrested after they stole a shipping container with the word BEEFEATERS across the front. These two must have thought they'd lucked out—a huge crate filled with bottles of premium gin that they could quickly and easily sell on the black market. The only problem with their plan was the *s*. What do I mean? Well, the name of the gin is Beefeater—without an *s*. So what did the thieves wind up stealing instead? Seven hundred and ninety-nine cases of toy dog bones. The owner of the dog-bone company, Steven Mendal, stated that this was the second robbery within two months by illiterate criminals. If anyone out there knows the street value of toy dog bones, I'm sure these fellows would like to know.

ROOM SERVICE

*P*olice in Portland, Oregon, received an emergency 911 call from a man staying at a local Howard Johnson Motel about mysterious intruders in his room. The thirty-three-year-old told the police that someone was trying to break into his second-floor room and hide under his bed. When the police arrived, the man jumped to the ground from the second floor and injured his back. The police searched his room but didn't find any intruders; what they did find was some heroin and cocaine. The man was taken to Brighton Medical Center for evaluation. I know the man was in possession of drugs, but it also sounded like he was possessed himself.

Police shot a man who was caught attempting to rob a grocery store after he charged them in an attempt to escape. According to the police, the man ran toward them with his index finger extended and yelled, "Bang! Bang!"

THE JOKE IS ON HIM

*C*ounterfeiting is a crime most people associate with criminals who have above-average intelligence and a certain level of skill. However, one Orlando, Florida, man's counterfeiting scheme went against that stereotype when he printed several million zlotys (Polish currency), for a total worth not more than $300. What put the man's black-market operation in the red was the fact that the machine he purchased to print the counterfeit zlotys cost $19,000. A Secret Service agent who was responsible for the arrest said, "He could have printed a boxcar full of them and not have enough to buy an expensive suit." The man won't have to worry about buying a suit for a while–because his clothes are now courtesy of the Florida prison system.

ARMED AND DANGEROUS

A bank robber carrying a crossbow, an ax, a stun gun, a smoke grenade, and a can of Mace walked into a bank in Osaka, Japan, and declared a holdup. He told the frightened tellers that he was prepared to use his entire arsenal if they didn't come across with the money. Fearing for their lives, the clerks gave the man $1,120,000; he grabbed it and made his escape. Unfortunately for the robber, but fortunately for the bank, the crook was so loaded down with weapons that he tripped and was quickly apprehended by a passerby. Too much of a good thing is a bad thing.

"I robbed from the rich, kind of like Robin Hood, except I kept it."

Career criminal Bill Becker summing up his life of crime.

THOSE ZANY, WACKY PRISONER LAWSUITS

- Jose Rivera Martinez, an inmate in Schenectady, New York, filed a $750,000 lawsuit against the county jail claiming he was allergic to the jail-issued hot dogs. His lawsuit alleged that the hot dogs he was forced to eat made him develop warts, which permanently disfigured him.

- Ernesto Mota filed a $7 million lawsuit claiming that the police in Oak Forest, Illinois, acted negligently after his arrest. Mota swallowed a bag of cocaine that was to be used as evidence against him, and subsequently suffered severe brain damage. He alleged that the police should have stopped him, or at least helped him receive medical attention more quickly.

- New York inmate David Degondea, who killed a police officer, filed a $3 million lawsuit seeking damages because he was injured during the arrest and could no longer work. Degondea's only source of income was selling drugs.

CAN'T WE JUST GET ALONG?

John Esposito, who was being held in the Suffolk County Correctional Center on Long Island for kidnapping, always felt like a pawn when he played chess with the prisoner in the next cell—alleged serial killer Joel Rifkin. Rifkin, who was linked to at least nineteen murders, and Esposito would challenge each other to chess matches through the bars of their adjoining cells, but Esposito always lost. Andrew Siben, Esposito's lawyer, checked the chess-playing escapades by telling his client, "It's not good for your morale to get beaten by a serial killer." And there's nothing worse than a kidnapper with low self-esteem.

In Columbia, Missouri, a man failed in his attempt to rob a grocery store using a socket wrench as his only weapon.

ACID REFLUX

*H*e was able to actualize himself up the tree but was not able to actualize himself down the tree" was the explanation given by High Point, North Carolina, police officer Gordon Snaden. The officer was referring to an incident involving a man who had ingested LSD and was found stranded naked in a tree.

PULL A HEIST AND PULL MY FINGER

A man and his wife were sleeping soundly in the bedroom of their Fire Island, New York, home when they heard noises in the house. They jumped out of bed to investigate, but although they thoroughly searched the house, they couldn't find the source of the noise. As they were preparing to go back to bed, they heard the unmistakable sound of flatulence coming from behind a closet door. They threw open the door and discovered a gaseous and bloated burglar hiding in the closet. They held the cramping career criminal, and their noses, until the police arrived. I don't know if they struck up a conversation, but I'll bet they struck a match.

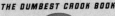
*A burglar in Union City, California,
was startled when the homeowner returned,
and dashed out of the house, over a fence,
and into a neighbor's yard. The burglar, who,
for some reason, was completely naked,
was quickly captured after his leap over
the fence landed him in the neighbor's
cactus garden.*

MAKING A BAD CALL

Some inmates, having so much time on their hands, find creative ways of whiling away the hours: they read or write books, file frivolous lawsuits, work out, make notes on their memoirs, learn a new occupation, and so on. But one curious inmate, serving time for a gas station robbery, was preoccupied with why he had never been prosecuted for a bank robbery for which he had previously been arrested and charged. The convict called the county attorney's office and asked about the oversight. The prosecutor did some research and discovered that the curious convict's file had been misplaced and that there were only a few months remaining before the statute of limitations ran out. The criminal, who was already serving ten years, plea-bargained with the DA to tack an additional ten years onto his sentence.

While attempting to rob a Long Island jewelry store at gunpoint, the 350-pound thief tripped and fell to the floor. He was still trying to get to his feet when the police arrived.

DRIVEN TO DISTRACTION

P olice in Lexington, North Carolina, arrived at the scene of a single-car accident and immediately arrested the three occupants. The men were charged with robbing a pedestrian and a gas station attendant just minutes before their accident. The accident was caused by the driver's attempt to make a speedy getaway while at the same time counting the stolen money.

GETTING SHORTCHANGED

*P*olice in Burlingame, California, were called out to investigate a burglary at the Towles Coffee Shop. The owners of the store kept things locked up after closing, and the burglar had had a hard time finding anything worth stealing. The police surmised that he'd made several attempts at breaking into a locked metal cabinet but was ultimately unsuccessful (the cabinet contained toilet paper anyway). Finally, not wanting to leave empty-handed and be the laughingstock of the burglary community, he stole the money from the "penny cup," which was located next to the cash register. The thief got away with about thirty cents in change. I hope he didn't spend it all in one place.

TWO WILL GET YOU TWENTY

Armed robbery is a serious offense, regardless of the amount of money or merchandise stolen, as two young criminals in Florence, Oregon, found out. They targeted a man and approached him with their weapons drawn, demanding money. The man claimed he was broke, so the two thieves settled for stealing a couple of cigarettes from the man. They were arrested, charged with armed robbery, and now face as much as twenty years behind bars. Once inside the jail the two shouldn't have any trouble finding as many cigarettes as they want.

Police in Long Hill Township, New Jersey, are on the lookout for a serial doorbell thief.

LANDING IN THE ROUGH

*P*olice helicopters were patrolling the skies looking for a man who had robbed a woman earlier in the day. The chase had been on for hours and the suspect had done a great job of eluding the police; his two accomplices, however, had already been captured. The Miami Shores, Florida, police captain said the man had the chance of being "the one guy that might have gotten away." Unfortunately, he was too polite. He was discovered by a stroke of luck—well, actually, a slice of luck. A golfer had sliced the ball off the tee and it had landed deep in the woods. As he was wandering around looking for his ball, he heard a voice from above: "Hey, hey, your ball is over there." The golfer looked up into a large tree and saw a man hiding among the branches. He quickly deduced from the helicopters searching the area that he should notify the police. He did, and when the police arrived, the man was more "up a tree" than he had been before. A lesson learned: keep your eye on the ball and your mouth shut.

BIRDBRAIN

A woman and a parrot walk into a bar. It sounds like the beginning of a joke, doesn't it? Well, in a sense it is. Patrons of a Minneapolis, Minnesota, bar watched as a woman entered the bar with a box under her arm. The woman opened the box and showed everyone a beautiful parrot, which she then offered to sell. One of the patrons looked in the box and remarked on the splendor and beauty of the parrot. The man knew all about this particular breed of parrot, he told her, because he had one at home that looked exactly like it. The man finished his drink and went back to his house only to discover that—you guessed it—his parrot was missing. He informed the police, who went back to the bar and discovered the woman still there and still trying to hock the bird. The man got his bird back and the woman got put in the cage.

An early-morning robbery of a Burger King
in Portland, Connecticut, ended abruptly when
the thief thought he heard an alarm go off
and left the store empty-handed. According to
the restaurant's manager, Jorge Ruisanchez,
the robber "disappeared in two seconds" after
hearing what turned out to be the timer
going off on the microwave oven.

ZERO PERCENT INTEREST

*T*he customers and staff of a bank in Ishioka, Japan, were unimpressed when a seventeen-year-old boy and his sixteen-year-old girlfriend brandished a pair of kitchen knives and threatened a holdup. The boy walked up to a customer and held out the knife, but the man shook his head and walked away. Our rebuffed robber then turned his attention to the teller and flashed his knife menacingly. The boy's girlfriend was disgusted at the poor job he was doing and started telling him so in no uncertain terms. The two cutlery-carrying criminals then got into a lovers' brawl in front of the entire bank. Their argument grew to such an intensity that they didn't notice that one teller had triggered the bank's silent alarm. When the police arrived, they found the young man standing in the middle of the bank, still wielding his knife and begging someone to please give him some money. His girlfriend was by then telling him to hurry it up.

MAKING A HOUSE CALL

In most cases a home robbery takes less than seven minutes, from the time the house is entered until the burglar leaves with your valuables. But in one case a burglar in Sandown, New Hampshire, realized he had some time on his hands and took advantage of it. The burglar literally made himself at home: he took a leisurely swim in the backyard pool, cooked himself a dinner of pork chops and Tater Tots, and loaded up the home-owner's truck with a BB gun and a watch. (Not a big haul–but who knows what stupidity lurks in the hearts of men?) Even with all the time spent on extracurricular activities, our "stay-at-home robber" nearly got away. The homeowner returned and caught the burglar trying in vain to get the truck started. He went from having a lot of time to serving a lot of time.

IT'S NOT AN INTELLIGENCE TEST

A man and woman arrested for the robbery of the Everett, Massachusetts, Co-op Bank were also suspects in at least eight other successful bank robberies. Getting a confession from the woman robber was easier than the police could have expected. According to Lieutenant Robert Botempo, "When I was booking this woman, I was asking her all the routine questions—you know: height, weight, age. For occupation, she said, 'Bank robber.'"

A twenty-four-year-old Texas man broke into a residence, stole a television set, and made a clean getaway. He was arrested a few hours later reentering the premises—he had forgotten to steal the television's remote control and came back to get it.

LIFE AIN'T SO BAD

*T*he hunt was on for an escaped murderer who had walked away from his minimum-security dormitory at the Chillicothe Correctional Institution in Ohio. The manhunt was in its second day when the police got a surprise tip. "We received a 911 phone call from [the escapee]. He said he was at a Shell station at I-71 and Route 35. He gave his name and birth date and said that he was the person we probably were looking for," Sheriff William R. Crooks said. Crooks and three deputies arrived at the service station and the exhausted escapee went quietly and without incident. "From the looks of him, he was tired, cold, and muddy," Crooks said. They sure don't make criminals the way they used to.

Two dim-witted thieves in Kazakhstan tried to steal valuable copper wire from an electricity cable in hopes of selling the metal on the black market. Although the men didn't escape, they will not be prosecuted for their offense— because they tried to steal the wire while the switch was on and ten kilovolts of electricity was surging through the line.

I'M SO BLUE

A man from Miami, Florida, was stopped by a patrol car under suspicion of driving while intoxicated and given a field sobriety test. He failed the test, but he claimed he wasn't drunk, so the police took him to headquarters to perform a Breathalyzer test. The supposedly sauced suspect asked if he could use the rest room before he took the Breathalyzer (apparently tests made him nervous), and the police agreed. After a longer than normal time the police entered the rest room to see if the man was all right. He wasn't. He was lying on the floor, jerking around, with blue foam spewing from his mouth. Was he having a bizarre seizure? Nope. Apparently the man ate a blue urinal deodorant cake, assuming it would cover up any telltale signs of alcohol on his breath. The man was taken to the hospital, where a blood test revealed that he had a blood-alcohol level beyond the legal limit, and he was arrested for DUI. There was no way this criminal could talk his way out of a jail sentence—even though he was already blue in the face.

YOUR BRAIN—
DON'T LEAVE HOME WITHOUT IT

A pair of burglars successfully broke into an insurance office in Golden, Colorado, and proceeded to help themselves to the company's computer equipment. It was hard and sweaty work, and as they hadn't set off the alarm, they decided to take their time going about their chores. One of the criminals took off his jacket and threw it over a chair while he was disconnecting monitors from hard drives, unplugging power cords, and preparing to haul off nearly $30,000 in equipment. The other criminal, seeing how well things were going, decided to call his ex-wife in New Jersey on the company line. After their rest time the two loaded up the van and took off with a large load of valuable equipment. The first crook was arrested the following day—he'd remembered to take all the computer stuff, but he'd forgotten his jacket, which contained his pay stub in the front pocket. The second criminal was caught a few days later—had his accomplice ratted him out in order to get leniency? Nope. When the insurance company received their monthly phone bill, there was a charge to New Jersey at 2:45 in the morning. They traced the call to the second thief's ex-wife and she cooperated fully with the police. Calling your ex-wife while you're burglarizing a business—it seems like this fellow was just asking for it, doesn't it?

THREE STRIKES AND YOU'RE OUT!

*A*n old saying claims, "There is honor among thieves." Having waded into the shallow end of the criminal gene pool in collecting stories for this book, I doubt that this statement has any basis in reality. But I suppose it could be considered true in the case of one convenience-store robber in Fort Collins, Colorado. You see, our criminal had already robbed the same 7-Eleven store twice in one day, once in the morning and once in the afternoon. Apparently he wasn't very original, because he told the clerk, as he was leaving the store after the second robbery, that he would return later in the day to rob the store again. He wanted to give the clerk a break in between robberies so there would be more money in the cash register. Here's where the honor part comes in: true to his word, the same man entered the same 7-Eleven with the same intent—to rob the store. The only thing different was that there were several detectives in the store investigating the man's second robbery. Our virtuous villain was arrested on two counts of robbery and one count of attempted robbery.

YOU MAY ALREADY BE A WINNER . . .

*I*t's not one of the most common criminal teams, and this husband and wife duo were definitely not your typical Bonnie and Clyde gangsters. But the manager and assistant manager of a service station were surprised when a man and woman entered the store, waved a gun in their faces, and threatened to rob the place. The man took the manager at gunpoint into the office, where the safe was located, while the woman stayed out front holding the assistant manager at bay. Making small talk during the robbery, the assistant manager told the woman about the great contest the store was sponsoring and said that if she completed an entry form, she might win a slew of valuable prizes. And that's just what she did. The woman quickly filled in the blanks, using her real name, address, and phone number, crossed her fingers for good luck, and handed the form to the assistant manager. The couple was sent on an all-expenses-paid trip—up the river.

CROSSING A LINE

*T*he police in Valley Springs, California, received a cellular-phone-call complaint from a motorist about a dangerous truck driver on the road. The motorist explained that the truck in front of him was crossing the centerline, driving erratically, swerving, and weaving back and forth. A patrol car spotted the truck in question and motioned for him to pull over. The trucker obliged and stopped his vehicle on the side of the road. The Good Samaritan who'd called in the complaint also pulled over and parked behind the truck. One police officer approached the truck slowly, making a note of the license plate and the driver number, then walked to the cab to talk with the driver. The trucker was very cooperative and showed absolutely no signs of being intoxicated or under the influence of narcotics. The police then decided to speak with the man who had called in the complaint, and that's when they found the real source of the problem. The driver of the car was intoxicated, very intoxicated; he registered at twice the legal limit. What the driver in his stupor didn't realize was that the truck was driving in a straight line—he was the one that was swerving all over the road. This is another reason why people shouldn't drink and dial.

FINGERED

A shoe designer from Tokyo was so desperate for money, or attention, that he decided to pull off a kidnapping. And he knew the perfect victim–himself. The man made several phone calls to his family and mailed eight threatening letters, demanding fifty million yen for his return. To let them know he meant business, in the seventh letter, he sent his left ring finger and a final threat that the kidnapper (himself) would kill him if they didn't pay the money. The thirty-six-year-old self-napper was arrested after the police got word that a man had entered the emergency room with his left ring finger missing. The police traced the fingerprints left at the hospital; they matched those of the fake kidnapper. This isn't the first time that a stupid criminal has fingered himself.

In Italy, a man who was sentenced to six years in jail for aggravated robbery escaped incarceration by fleeing the country. After two years on the lam the man was arrested after he reentered his country. He was asked by the authorities why he'd risked arrest by returning to Italy; the man confessed that he had "missed the pizza."

HE WAS JUST A FIFTH WHEEL

A drug dealer in Jacob Lake, Arizona, found himself stranded on the side of the highway after his car broke down. He flagged down a passing truck driver, who was kind enough to pull his rig off the road and offer the stranded motorist a ride. The man said he didn't want to leave all of his personal items in the car for fear they would be stolen and asked if he could take some stuff with him in the truck's cab. The driver said he understood completely—you can't trust anyone these days. The motorist was thankful, and in a few minutes he was back with his arms filled with stuff: some clothes, a shaving kit, some of this and some of that, and, of course, a spare tire. The man insisted that he needed to bring along the spare tire and asked the truck driver just to drop him off at a local motel. The driver pulled into the motel parking lot and watched as the man walked toward his room, rolling the spare tire in front of him. Now, people have taken strange things inside their motel rooms before, but a spare tire got the driver's attention and he thought he would bring it to the attention of the police. The police, upon inspecting the tire, found eleven pounds of marijuana hidden inside it. Now the drug dealer had better hope he's got another kind of spare—spare time, that is, and lots of it.

A FAMILY GATHERING

Robert Palmer was arrested and charged with burglary in Savannah, Georgia, after removing a windowpane and entering the residence of Joseph Palmer. When the police detained him, he claimed he hadn't planned to rob the place; he was only curious as to whether he and Joseph Palmer were related. They're not.

A man held up a Toronto, Ontario, gas station wearing a pair of women's panties over his head to hide his identity. He was quickly apprehended because in order to make himself heard by the clerk, he stuck his face through one of the leg openings.

A DAY LATE AND A DOLLAR SHORT

A twenty-four-year-old Detroit Lakes, Minnesota, man was arrested and charged with the attempted robbery of a convenience store. According to prosecutors, the robber wanna-be stopped a customer on his way into the store and handed him a dollar. The criminal told the man he intended to rob the store but didn't have a proper disguise and asked if the fellow would be so kind as to buy him a handkerchief that he could use to hide his face. The man took the dollar, walked into the store, and told the clerk about the odd encounter outside, and the clerk notified the police. No mention about what happened to the dollar.

AN OPEN-AND-SHUT CASE

A young would-be car thief broke into a garage in Waskom, Texas, and snuck into the owner's van with the intention of stealing it. Apparently the thief wasn't mechanically inclined, because as he was fumbling around trying to hot-wire the car, he accidentally activated the electric locks–and couldn't find the right button to open them. He was making so much noise frantically pushing every button he could find to open the door that he woke the owners. When the police arrived, they found the suspect still locked in the van. And with this type of criminal mentality a prison escape is entirely unlikely.

A market in Greensboro, North Carolina, was robbed by two men—one of them brandishing a pitchfork.

THE CHECK'S IN THE JAIL

A man in Auburn, California, was arrested and charged with burglary, forgery, and passing bad checks after purchasing $267 worth of supplies from an office store. The man had painstakingly printed bogus checks, complete with false bank account numbers that could successfully be scanned through any store's "check identification" system. So where did our crafty counterfeiter go wrong? For some unknown reason, the man had printed his full and proper name and address on every check. Pay to the order of: Idiot.

One career criminal was killed when he and another man got into a fight over who had the longest criminal record.

RUN FOR COVER

An Angolan man had the patrons and staff of a Madrid, Spain, café trembling as he shouldered his weapon and looked down the barrel. It was a daring midday robbery, and the armed man had the drop on everyone, demanding their money lest he open fire on them. It was then that an observant waiter recognized the make and model of the weapon the robber had— it was a 1998 black umbrella. "At first, people thought it was a rifle and then a waiter noticed it was a fake," a police spokesperson said. Waiters rushed the dumb-fella with the umbrella and quickly disarmed him.

A man stole a vehicle from the Hastings,
Nebraska, city storage shed and drove it to a
local convenience store to buy a case of beer.
Upon arriving at the store the man paid for the
beer and filled up the vehicle with gas before
returning home. The clerk, suspecting that the
man was drunk, alerted the police and described
both the man and the vehicle. A few days before,
the city had experienced a major snowstorm, and
our drunk driver had stolen the only thing he
knew would get him to the store—a snowplow.

THE REAL MR. MONEYBAGS

Robbing an armored truck is a very dangerous heist; the guards are heavily armed, and the truck is virtually impenetrable. But an armored truck in Memphis, Tennessee, was successfully robbed as the truck guard was about to enter a supermarket to make a pickup. Two gunmen approached him, put their guns in the driver's face, took the large canvas bag he was carrying, and made their getaway. The bag was fairly light, but it was definitely filled with something. The crooks stopped a short distance away to check out their booty and were sadly disappointed. Remember, the guard was making a pickup, so the only thing stuffed in the large canvas moneybag . . . was a stack of other large canvas moneybags.

THE FAT OF THE LAND

The getaway is one of the most important parts of any successful bank robbery. One needs to have the proper vehicle ready and running, make sure there's gas in the tank, have a fairly well planned escape route, and so on. But one robber thought he would just wing his escape–or, actually, foot it. A man in Fremont, California, had accomplished the first part of a bank robbery–the initial "Give me all the money" bit. He took the money and headed out the door intending to run "wee, wee, wee" all the way home. Passersby, who saw the man exit the bank with the money, however, had a different idea and gave chase. After less than a block the robber gave up his sprint to freedom and slowed down to a leisurely walk. Was he confident that he had gotten away? Nope. You see, the suspect was only five foot six and weighed well over three hundred pounds. Our rotund robber needed a rest, and the sentencing judge was more than glad to give him several years to catch his breath.

A shoplifter at the Tom Tom CDs & Tapes Store in St. George, Utah, was seen stuffing a CD under his shirt and was stopped by the clerk. The thief tore free, bolted through the door, and ran face-first into a pillar in front of the store, knocking himself unconscious.

DON'T BE A LITTERBUG

*C*ops in a patrol car in Los Angeles observed a vehicle swerving on and off the road, crossing the centerline, and driving very erratically over all. They popped on the lights and began pursuit. When the driver of the car realized the police were hot on his tail, he tried to throw a beer can out the window—an obvious sign that the man was very intoxicated. He was so intoxicated, in fact, that he had a hard time getting the can through the window. He thought the logical thing to do would be to make the opening bigger—so he opened his car door in order to throw the can out. He was successful in tossing the can out of the speeding car; he just forgot to let go of it. The man bounced down the road but was left with only minor scrapes and bruises . . . no word on the condition of the beer can.

A man who was suffering from amnesia asked the police in Hamburg, Germany, to help him find out his identity. He wished he hadn't done that when the police discovered that he was wanted for fraud and arrested him.

NOTHING RUNS LIKE A DEER

Not unlike the previous story, this is a police chase that will go down in the annals of stupid-criminal history. A man from Gastonia, North Carolina, stole a vehicle and made his get-away. He knew the cops would pursue him, so he wanted to make sure he had a full tank of gas. His first stop was a local gas station, where he filled up the tank and then committed his second crime by not paying for the gas. The driver put the pedal to the metal and hit the road, pushing the limits of the engine in order to put distance between him and the coppers. There was a gap of thirty minutes between the first crime of stealing the vehicle and the second crime of stealing the gas before the police were alerted to the criminal's activities by a call from the gas station attendant. They jumped in their patrol cars, strapped on their seat belts, hit the blue lights, and sped out of the parking lot. They soon spotted the man, as he had pulled the stolen vehicle off the road and was now driving down the sidewalk. The police cut in front of the man and forced him to stop and kill the ignition. Why did the chase last such a short time? Well, the vehicle the man had stolen was a bright red Troy-Bilt riding lawn mower. The man was arrested and charged with stealing the lawn mower and the gas and resisting arrest. Of course, he might make a deal with the judge to trim his sentence.

HITTING THE WRONG NOTE

*K*evin McCarthy, a clerk at a Check Exchange, taught one would-be robber that a copy of Strunk and White's *The Elements of Style* is a crucial resource manual when preparing a proper holdup note. The clerk became suspicious of the man when he first saw him pacing outside the exchange. "Before he came in, I thought he was a funny-looking guy, with a dark wig, a funny glue-on mustache, glue-on sideburns, a long dark coat, a baseball cap, and a duffel bag. He handed me a Western Union slip that was just a bunch of gibberish. I didn't even try to read it—it was just ridiculous," McCarthy said. "I was just about to tell him, 'You'll have to rewrite this,' when he pulled out a shoe box with some red sticks that looked like dynamite inside." The irate illiterate thrust the note back at the clerk, who was seated comfortably behind inch-thick bulletproof glass, and asked, "Can you read that?" "I said no and hit the alarm button," recalled McCarthy. The man stormed out of the exchange swearing loudly—he was not apprehended. No one is sure whether the shoe box contained dynamite or flares, but one thing is certain: the man definitely had a short fuse.

CHOKING ON HIS OWN WORDS

A man convicted of kidnapping and robbery tried to get his sentence overturned by claiming that the witnesses' identification of him shouldn't have been entered at the trial. When the New Haven, Connecticut, police officers arrested the man, he declared himself innocent of all charges and asked to be released. However, he resisted going back for a "one-on-one face-off," a procedure in which the suspected criminal is brought to the scene of the crime for identification purposes. The man claimed it was a waste of time to take him back, because he was innocent; furthermore, he stated, "How can they identify me? I had a mask on."

A man robbed a post office in Cariato, Italy, and made off with L3,000. He ran outside and discovered that his getaway car, which he had left running, had been stolen.

A SIX-PACK SHY OF A CASE

An inebriated man in Longmont, Colorado, had just finished off his third six-pack but still had a thirst for more brew. So he jumped into his car and drove to the same convenience store where he had bought his original three sixers–I suppose he wanted to make it an even case. When he got there, he had the idea of getting the beer at a discount: a five-fingered discount. So he got out a crowbar and started working drunkenly on the front door, trying to pry it open, but even through his hazy, bloodshot eyes, he could tell something was wrong–the store was still open. Customers inside the store stared in amazement at the man working feverishly to open the door and, thinking he might need some help, they called the police. Once the man realized his mistake, he tried to make his escape, but search as he might he couldn't find the keys to his car. The police arrived and allowed the man to sober up in jail. It turned out that the reason he couldn't find his keys was that he had left them in the ignition.

A PATTY SHY OF A WHOPPER

It was shortly before eight in the morning when a man entered a Burger King in Ypsilanti, Michigan, and pulled out a gun. He demanded all the cash in the fast-food store and demanded it fast (and I'm not talking thirty minutes or less). The clerk explained that the drawers wouldn't open without a food order. So the robber asked for a burger and a side of onion rings. "Sorry," the clerk said, pointing to the clock, "those items are only sold after ten-thirty." Either not in the mood for breakfast or tired of not having things his way, the man pocketed the gun and slumped out of the store. Hold the pickles, hold the lettuce, special orders do upset us.

A robbery duo in Michigan entered a record shop and spastically waved their pistols. The first robber shouted, "Nobody move!" He noticed movement out of the corner of his eye and fired—shooting his fidgety partner.

HE WAS DUMB—TO COIN A PHRASE

A man broke into a rare-coin shop and looked in amazement at the different sizes and shapes of coins set out in display cabinets throughout the store. He needed to know which coins were worth the most, as it would help him set a price when he resold them. He spotted a book detailing the various grades and values of rare coins and picked it up, had a seat, and started thumbing through the volume. I suppose a book about old coins must be pretty boring, because soon the man fell fast asleep. That's how the police found him the next morning . . . sleeping soundly with the book of coin values lying open on his lap. The man, like some of the coins he had been reading about, was taken out of circulation.

HANDBAGGED

A woman in Stratford, Ontario, was in a supermarket doing a little shopping for women's wallets–other women's wallets. The woman looked innocent enough, strolling around the supermarket with a shopping cart, but her eyes weren't on produce but on purses. She would wait until an unsuspecting shopper was looking the other way and then quickly relieve her of her wallet. She soon felt she was under surveillance and decided to take the stolen wallets out of her purse, throw all four of them into a waste bin, and leave the store. At home, the woman breathed a sigh of relief as she settled onto her couch to watch a little television. She got up to answer a knock at the door and was surprised to find the police there to arrest her for robbery. How had they tracked her down? It turns out the woman had stolen only three wallets that day–the fourth wallet she'd thrown away was her own.

A young woman in Lake City, Florida, was arrested for attempting to hold up a Howard Johnson Motel with a chain saw. Fortunately for the clerk, the chain saw was electric . . . and wasn't plugged in.

HI-HO, QUICKSILVER, AWAY!!!

*T*wo young men in Texarkana, Arkansas, became big hits with their friends when they showed up with a shiny, silver-white liquid that looked really cool. The boys played with the magic liquid, watching in amazement as it beaded up on their arms when they dipped them into the container, then poured it on the floor and stared as it shimmered and danced. When asked where they got such great stuff, the boys answered that they'd stolen it from an abandoned neon-sign plant. They had several containers of the liquid, and they said they would gladly share it with their friends. What the boys didn't realize was that the liquid was highly poisonous mercury—used in the production of neon signs. The two were arrested for breaking and entering, and their little idiotic experiments forced the evacuation of ten homes, the temporary closing of their high school, the medical treatment of more than sixty people, and the shutting down of a Subway sandwich shop. It's interesting that the boys stole mercury, which is, of course, named after the Greek god Mercury . . . who is the god of travel, commerce, and thievery.

THE THREE STOOGES

*I*t was a plan intended to make them all millionaires–a great con, they thought; a clever scam, they giggled; a dumb idea, actually. Three inmates at New York's Rikers Island Prison worked in tandem to hatch a plot to smuggle a gun inside the prison walls. One of the inmates had a day job and was able to successfully bring the loaded weapon onto the prison grounds and into his cell. Were they planning on breaking out? Nope. Here's the plot: One of the inmates would take the gun the other inmate brought in and shoot the third inmate in the leg. The wounded inmate would then sue the prison for "negligence" in allowing a gun to be smuggled into the prison in the first place. They would then, as part of their settlement agreement, all be released from prison and collect "millions" in damages. Did it work? Part of it did–the part where one inmate shoots another in the leg. But the lawsuit never made it to trial, all three men are still behind bars, and one of them is now called Gimpy.

LOWERING THE BAR

A man who was recently released on bail for an armed robbery was looking for some fast cash to support his drug habit. He lived in a small apartment just above a tavern and thought that of all the places to hold up, the bar would require the least amount of effort. The man entered the darkly lighted Philadelphia bar with his gun drawn, went to the bartender, and demanded the day's take from the register. The bartender quickly obliged, handing him all the cash. The man took the money and ran back upstairs to his apartment. Ten minutes later, a knock on the door revealed to the man, who was sitting at the kitchen table counting his money, that he had already been tracked down. His main problem? Not only did he live upstairs from the bar, but also the bartender was his landlord, who, of course, had no trouble identifying the man and giving the police his current address.

DUMB ON ALL ACCOUNTS

We are all concerned about terrorists, bomb scares, and threats to our airlines–but if all terrorists were as stupid as this guy, we wouldn't have a care in the world. A South Carolina man claimed he had planted bombs at the airport terminals in both Columbia and Charleston and demanded $2 million to disclose their location, or else he would detonate them. He had obviously seen movies where undercover police officers stake out the area where the money drop-off occurs, so our "mad bomber" thought he would outsmart the police by changing the scenario. He told the authorities to deposit the $2 million in cash in his bank account, giving them the name of his bank and his account number. The police had no problem tracking down the address of the man who owned the bank account, and they made an arrest within minutes. The police did make a deposit, however; they deposited the man in the local jail.

FIRST COME, FIRST SERVED

*I*t was a "meet the police" night in a Spokane, Washington, community and people were getting to know their local police officers while examining some of the latest in crime-fighting and law-enforcement technology. One new product on display was a driver's license computer connected directly to the state's main computer. The new technology, the demonstrating officer promised, could run a check using your driver's license and automatically bring up any outstanding tickets. To prove that it worked, he asked for volunteers. One guy came forward, whipped out his driver's license, smiled to the crowd, and waited as the officer ran his number through the new system. Well, the computer worked, all right. It showed that the vacuum-headed volunteer was a wanted criminal with several outstanding warrants for his arrest. The phrase "meet the police" had a different meaning to the man, as they arrested him on the spot.

A judge looked at his docket and called the next case: *PEOPLE VS. STEVEN LEWON CROOK.* When the judge was ready to see the defendant, he called, "Crook, come forward." Five prisoners left the holding cell and entered the courtroom.

A Nevada man who was wanted on outstanding warrants for fraud decided to make a new life for himself when he reached West Haven, Connecticut. As his first step in walking the straight and narrow, he applied for a job and was summarily arrested. Why? The position he applied for was with the local police department, which uncovered his record during a routine background check.

UNDER WHERE?

The police in Klamath Falls, Oregon, received a call from a homeowner who had just been the victim of a robbery. Two officers responded immediately and took the statement of the homeowner. The victim said a man had broken into his house, knocked him to the floor, stolen several items from his home, and then left—and oh, by the way, the thief was only wearing his underwear. Apparently the robber had removed his pants and shirt in the homeowner's front yard before entering the house, under the assumption that it would be harder to identify him. In his haste to escape, the underwear-wearing robber had forgotten to take the shirt and pants he had left in the front yard. When the police examined the pants, they found, in the back pocket, the man's wallet and photo ID. So the man's robbery attire and his career as a thief were the same: brief.

A man robbed a liquor store in the Roswell area of New Mexico. Although he wore a bag over his head, the police got an excellent description of the perpetrator—he was wearing a plastic bag.

A SURPRISE ATTACK

*I*t was nice outside and we decided to open up the front door," Jeff Broxon said. Jeff and his wife, Melane, put up a baby fence in their front door so their two dogs couldn't get out but they could still enjoy the weather. "I was sitting in a recliner drinking iced tea and my wife had just sat down on the couch with a bowl of ice cream." That's when it happened. Suddenly, a robber in a paper-bag mask leaped through the open front door of the Bradenton, Florida, home intending to surprise the couple inside and rob them. But the surprise was on him. "This guy comes jumping over this gate with a bag over his head," Jeff Broxon recalled. "He had a paper bag over his head with holes cut in it so he could see. He had a shirt over his arm like he was covering a gun, and he said, 'I'm going to blow your heads off if you don't give me your money.' I said, 'Okay, no problem.'"

Broxon carefully moved to one side and took out his wallet; he slowly opened it to reveal the contents to the would-be robber.

"I opened [the wallet] to draw attention away from my wife," he said.

Skeeter, one of the Broxons' dogs, provided further distraction by "running all over the place" and snapping at the robber's leg.

The intruder was so busy fighting off the dog and ogling the money in Broxon's wallet that he didn't notice that Melane had pulled out a .22-caliber pistol and had it pointed at his head.

Jeff smiled, the crook looked confused, Skeeter barked, and Melane kept the robber in her sights. "I looked at him and I said, 'Bud, I think you've had a bad day,'" Jeff said. "My wife had a gun pointed right at him," he continued. "She said, 'Freeze or you're dead.'"

Melane instructed the bandit to take off his mask and sit down on the floor with his hands on his knees. Jeff took the gun and Melane called 911. A few minutes later six carloads of police officers squealed in and arrested the unwanted guest.

"It was an interesting little evening," Jeff Broxon said. "The bad part of it was, we missed the end of the program we were watching." I've seen television lately, and I can't think of any show that would have been more interesting or more entertaining than that.

CALLING ALL CARS

*A*s the speeding car raced away from the scene of a Portland, Oregon, bank robbery, one alert citizen wrote down the number of the car's license plate. The police traced the number to what turned out to be the previous owner of the car—a man who, in fact, had sold the car to someone else earlier that year. The previous owner called the current owner and told him the police were asking questions about the whereabouts of the vehicle. In an unexplainable act of stupidity, the man who owned the car (a.k.a. "the Bank Robber") called the police to see what the problem might be. He told them that he was the current owner of the car and even gave them his correct street address—after which he was arrested for two bank robberies in the Portland area. The man was caught after the police put a make on his license plate, and now it'll be his responsibility to make license plates.

A man applying for a position at a Baltimore police station was handed the standard application form to fill out. On most job questionnaires there is a line about whether you've ever committed a crime. The man checked the "yes" box, and when asked by the officer in charge about his crime, the man admitted to carjacking a woman and robbing five people in Texas. Needless to say, he was arrested.

WARNING: NOT INTENDED AS A CHILD'S TOY

Employees of the First Bank and Trust Co., in Princeton, Kentucky, were going about their business when a man approached one of the tellers, waved a pistol, and demanded all the money in the till. The teller looked at the robber's face and knew he was serious; then she looked at the weapon he was pointing and realized that he was seriously stupid, too. The man was brandishing a plastic toy gun. The teller refused to give the man anything except the cold shoulder. While he was arguing with this teller, another employee of the bank, who happened to have a Polaroid camera handy, took a picture of the robber. After he was caught on candid camera, the man backed away from the counter and said he was just kidding—he was actually there to get change for a hundred-dollar bill. When the police were taking the man away, they noticed a rolled-up stocking underneath his baseball cap; he had forgotten to pull it down over his face before the robbery. Even though the weapon was plastic, the man was still charged with armed robbery.

SHUTTING OUT THE BAD ELEMENTS

*I*t was shortly after closing time at an Office Depot in Lennox, California, when a man who had been hiding in the store for an unknown amount of time came out of nowhere and declared he was going to rob the store. He hustled all the employees into an office and felt a sense of pride, knowing that everything was going according to plan, as he locked them securely away. He then quickly reviewed the steps of the plan: 1) Hide in the store–did that! 2) Get all the employees locked in an office–did that! 3) Open door, let partner in–that's next! 4) Clean out the place, ha, ha, ha. (Author's note: I made up that laugh part.) Seeing that he was at stage three, he trotted over to the back door, walked outside, and gave his buddy the all-clear sign. Of course, what he didn't notice was the ALL DOORS LOCK AUTO-MATICALLY sign on the inside of the door. Try as he might, he couldn't get back into the store. It's a clear-cut example of an open-and-shut case of stupidity.

Run for the Border: A bicycle bandit pedaled his bike to the drive-through window at a Fort Worth, Texas, Taco Bell and placed his order. He wanted all the money in the store . . . and a chalupa.

A YEN FOR MONEY

A man who was concerned about violating the terms of his driver's license, suspension from an earlier DUI case, decided not to drive his car to his next job. His next job, however, was the attempted robbery of the Shanghai Express Restaurant in Tampa, Florida. The conscientious criminal walked up to the drive-through window and demanded all the money in the restaurant—to go. When a car pulled up behind him at the window, the frightened fleet-footed felon fled. He was cornered a few blocks away by the police and given "free delivery" to the local jail.

I'M NOT WHO I THINK I AM

The police in Springfield, Illinois, pulled a young man over and cited him for driving without a license. When the officer asked him his name, the young man answered, "Johnny Rice." The officer was a little suspicious and asked the man to spell it for him–but the driver couldn't spell "Johnny" in any of the conventional ways. He then changed his mind and told the officer his real name. The police followed up on the suspicious fellow and contacted the car's owner. The owner of the car said that he had in fact loaned his friend the car and wasn't sure why he'd given the police a false name. A search was run on the man (using his real name, of course), and it turned out there were no warrants for his arrest and he wasn't wanted by the police on any matter–in fact, he had a clean record. Why he'd decided to give the officers a false name is something only, uh, only what's-his-name can answer.

GETTING A JUMP START ON A ROBBERY

Glenn Doolin, a tobacco farmer, pulled into his driveway, got out of his truck, and noticed two unfamiliar faces coming out of his house carrying some very familiar things—his stereo, compound bow, BB gun, and a pillowcase filled with jewelry. "I hollered at them, but they just kept on," Doolin said. "They never answered and then they got into their car. . . . When their car wouldn't start, they asked me if I wanted my stuff back, and they started unloading the stuff." Doolin was amazed and angered at seeing his possessions in the hands of someone else. "They started begging me not to call the police," Doolin said, but he did anyway. "Then they'd go back out and try to start the car, and the car wouldn't start, so they'd come back in and start begging. They must have done this four or five times," Doolin said. The stranded suspects finally asked Doolin if he would give their getaway car a jump start. Knowing their car was stalled, Doolin stalled the two thieves by saying he didn't have jumper cables but he'd run next door to borrow some. Then the hard-working farmer looked at the two men who were trying to take his possessions and decided to give them a piece of his mind. "I said, 'What's the matter with you?' I said, 'Look what you've done to the place.'" Doolin's pointed remarks got him something he didn't expect to see . . . his own loaded revolver pointed at his face. "I thought he was going to shoot me, but he just took the bullets from the gun and threw them out in the yard, and he said, 'Now we've done everything we can. . . . We'll even clean the place up.'" They began tidying up Doolin's house, begging him not to file a police report when the police arrived. Before they were hauled off, Doolin's curiosity got the best of him. He asked the robbers why they didn't run into the woods or take his truck, which still had the keys in the ignition, and even why they didn't shoot him to make their getaway. The two turned to look at the older man and said they weren't out to make a profit on the robbery. "They said they were just trying to steal enough to fix their car," recalled Doolin.

HE'S NOT SHARP ENOUGH TO CUT WARM BUTTER

A clerk working behind a lottery counter in Rochester Hills, Michigan, was threatened by a robber wielding a knife. Since the counter was between the two men, the clerk simply took a step back to be out of the way of the sharp knife and called security. The robber gave up, dropped the knife, and ran out of the store. Within minutes both the neighborhood and the store were swarming with police officers searching for the armed-robbery suspect. As the old saying goes, a criminal always returns to the scene of the crime, and it was true in this case, too. The man reentered the store a half hour later and asked if he could please have his knife back. He was tackled by security officers and arrested for attempted robbery. Why did the man risk arrest for a knife? Was it special? An antique? Nope. According to police sergeant Dennis Nash, "It was just a little paring knife." A paring knife isn't always the sharpest knife in the drawer—and neither was this guy.

WEIGHT AND SEE

*O*n Christmas Day a few years ago, a man called 911 and stopped a burglary in progress . . . he was an eyewitness to what was happening, because he was the burglar. Apparently the man walked into a health center and hid in a bathroom until the business closed for the night. Much to his chagrin, he soon realized that the valuable equipment and medicines were locked up—so he started jamming office supplies into his pockets. Then a thought occurred to him: "If they locked the doors, how am I going to get out?" He couldn't. So he picked up the phone and called 911, telling them he had been "buzzed" into the building to use the bathroom and the guard had forgotten he was there and closed up for the night. There was only one problem: the building had no buzzer security system. The building did, however, have an alarm system, which the burglar had accidentally set off twice. Each time he'd answered the phone call from the security guard and told him everything was okay. Police officer Deborah Reinarman said the man confessed to her that he regretted calling 911 for help. "He said he should have just broken a window," she reported. Too bad the bewildered burglar hadn't called her earlier for advice.

A grocery-store robbery in Calgary, Alberta, was hindered because of two things: 1) the robber's only weapon was an ordinary manual can opener; and 2) during the attempted getaway, the sixteen-month-old baby of the robber's girlfriend kept falling out of the stroller.

TAKE-OUT SERVICE

A St. Louis man who'd had a little too much to drink thought he would get something to eat and pulled his car up to what he thought was a drive-through restaurant. He drove up to the intercom and yelled his order. He soon realized that he'd ordered up a large portion of trouble—the man was yelling into the intercom of the Area III St. Louis police station. An officer came out, not wanting to see if the man wanted fries, but to see how fried he was—and arrested the driver for DUI. It's a good thing the man didn't ask to supersize it!

The follow-up on this story is that the next day a local radio DJ, "Wacky Pat" Fortune, wanting to play a prank for his listening audience, pulled up to the same intercom stand. A quick computer trace found that Fortune had several unpaid traffic tickets, and he was promptly arrested. ("Wacky"—yes; "Fortune"—no.)

I'M READY FOR MY CLOSE-UP, MR. DEMILLE

A man who considered himself an expert safecracker broke into a small Bloomington, Indiana, business he knew kept more than $7,000 in cash. He had checked out the place previously, and since it didn't have a burglar alarm and the safe was an older model, the crook thought the heist would be a cakewalk. As he was working away at the safe, he noticed a small red light shining from the corner of the ceiling and realized immediately that it was a surveillance camera. Our safecracker thought he'd take a crack at disabling the camera instead of trying to hide his identity. He climbed up on a chair, pulled out a screwdriver from his collection of safecracking tools, and removed the camera from its brackets. He then jumped off the chair, opened the safe, and took off with both the camera and the money. The only thing the criminal forgot was that the camera was connected to a tape deck in the office—so although he got away with the camera, he left an extremely good close-up of his face on the videotape. Remember: when you focus your attention on a project, make sure something isn't focused on you.

An inmate in the Auburn Hills, Michigan, jail was able to escape and left a note bragging to the authorities. The note read, "By the time you read this, I'll be halfway to Europe." Before the day was over, the man was back in his cell, having been caught a mere three miles away.

A BANK NOTE

A robber who apparently had a fear of public speaking composed a two-page holdup letter and presented it to the teller at a Des Moines, Iowa, bank. The teller looked over the letter and told the robber that although she knew it was a holdup, she was having a hard time understanding the writing. She asked if she could get another teller to help her decipher the letter. One of the details the teller had trouble with was the fact that the note demanded $19 trillion; that, she told the robber, would be impossible, as the bank didn't have that much cash in the vault. The robber agreed to allow the teller to gain the assistance of another teller to help with the letter. When the other teller arrived, the robber said he realized that the letter was a little convoluted, although it had taken him two weeks to write, and that they should take their time reading it. He told them he would wait outside while they read the letter and have a cigarette so as not to violate bank policy by smoking inside the lobby. He mentioned, on his way out, that if he wasn't finished with his smoke by the time they bagged up the $19 trillion, they could just bring it to him. The manager of the bank and the tellers agreed that the man was probably harmless, but he had threatened to rob the bank, so they alerted the police. In order to stall the man, a security guard went outside to tell him that his demands were being considered. The police arrived shortly afterward and placed the man under arrest without incident. The only comment the robber had was, "I guess they denied my robbery request! They probably couldn't come up with the nineteen trillion. I would have settled for a hundred million!" What he did was settle for a lot less money and a lot more time.

SHARP KNIFE, DULL ROBBER

*A*n out-of-shape criminal from Sudbury, Ontario, was arrested and charged with the attempted robbery of a candy store. The easily winded robber entered the store, pulled out an X-Acto knife, and threatened the clerk with it. The clerk, unfazed by the small razor, picked up the phone and called 911 while the thief watched. When the police arrived, the box-cutter bandit was still in the store. Asked why he hadn't tried to make a break for it, the slow sneak thief replied, "I can't run too fast." The police were kind enough to give the poor man a lift–to police headquarters.

Two men in Loveland, Colorado, were arrested for robbing a pet store—for some reason they had stolen five hedgehogs.

BY ANY MEANS POSSIBLE

The owner of a Ford Probe was waiting at a traffic light when a man came out of nowhere, put a knife to his throat, demanded the car, pushed him out, and drove away. The car thief had only driven a short distance when he collided with a pickup truck, totaling the car. Now he knew he was really in trouble–not only had he stolen a car, but he was about to be guilty of a hit-and-run. The criminal quickly looked around for another mode of transportation and found a hot little pink-and-white number and took off. When the police apprehended him, he claimed he was the rightful owner of the set of wheels and was simply on his way home. The police doubted the man's explanation, because his new getaway vehicle was a little girl's bicycle. The man was caught furiously pedaling away from the scene and was charged with, among other things, two counts of larceny: one for the car and one for the bike. Look, Ma . . . no brains.

IT DOESN'T ALWAYS PAY TO ADVERTISE

*A*n inmate at the San Mateo County, California, minimum-security jail decided he'd had enough of prison life and simply strolled away during work release. He got a little tired of walking after a while and stopped at a pay phone to call a friend to come pick him up. But try as he might, the convict couldn't remember his friend's phone number, so he called directory assistance to get it. Unfortunately, he accidentally dialed 911 instead of 411, then quickly hung up the phone when a dispatcher answered. The police sent out a cruiser to check on the 911 hang-up anyway and found the man still in the phone booth and still wearing his prison shirt, with the words PROPERTY OF SAN MATEO COUNTY HONOR CAMP written on it. "They could see it through the top of his jacket," Sheriff's lieutenant Larry Boss said. At least when they took the inmate back to celebrate his reunion with his fellow prisoners, he was already dressed for the occasion.

NEXT TIME, FOCUS YOUR ATTENTION

*T*wo men in San Diego were arrested for burglary when a camera they had stolen turned them in. Here's what happened. The police were investigating one of the men on a separate charge and noticed a new video camera in the man's apartment. The man didn't have a receipt for the camera, and he couldn't give a believable explanation of how it had come into his possession. The police confiscated the video camera, and after they'd watched the tape, they arrested the man and his accomplice and charged them with burglary. Among the scenes on the videotape was one, shot at an extremely odd angle, showing the two men congratulating each other on a burglary well done, flaunting some of the merchandise they had stolen, and complimenting themselves on being smart enough not only to steal the video camera but also to remember to take the instruction manual. Unfortunately, the two had never read the manual and had inadvertently turned the camera on and left it on a table when they were celebrating their burglary success. Smile, you're on *Candid Camera*.

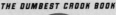

During a picnic of county probation officers in Yuba City, California, two thieves failed in their attempt to steal a barbecue grill—the grill was still hot.

THERE'LL BE TIME ENOUGH FOR COUNTIN' WHEN THE DEALIN'S DONE

A man entered a Baltimore, Maryland, branch of Signet Bank, walked straight to the teller, and handed her a note. The note demanded money, and the teller, as trained, gave the robber the cash without any static. She then set off the silent alarm that alerts the local police station. The police always respond quickly to a bank-robbery alarm; they occasionally catch the criminal within a short distance of the bank but certainly don't expect to get there before the robber leaves. Only that's what happened in this case. You see, after the man received the money, he walked over to a nearby counter and began counting his haul. He was still in the process of tallying his take when the police took him away.

A TWO-BIT DRILL THIEF

A Builders Square store in Homewood, Illinois, was busy as usual, with people shopping for merchandise to improve their homes. A man stood in the checkout line with other *Tool Time* buddies, and when it was his turn, placed an electric drill on the counter. The man reached into his wallet and pulled out a hundred-dollar bill, which the clerk ran through a counterfeit-detection device. The bill came up as being genuine, and as the clerk was putting the drill in a bag, the customer pulled out a gun and demanded all the cash in the register. The clerk quickly obliged and handed the man the entire contents—ninety-five dollars. The man took the money and left the store. Sounds like a successful robbery, right? Well, it would have been if the man hadn't left both his original hundred-dollar bill and the drill on the counter. I wonder if the clerk was allowed to keep the five dollars as a tip?

A man in Wilmington, North Carolina, was arrested and charged with theft after he dug up and stole fifteen hundred Venus flytraps.

SMALL-CHANGE ARTIST

*T*he police in Corpus Christi, Texas, think they've finally found the man responsible for a string of gumball-machine thefts in the area, after the suspect's landlord tipped off the authorities to the man's whereabouts. The landlord became suspicious of the man when he went to his apartment to collect the rent and saw a massive pile of jawbreakers on the floor. But what really clued the landlord in was the fact that the man routinely paid his weekly rent entirely in quarters. Gives a whole new meaning to the phrase "living quarters."

During a police lineup, the detective told each man to step forward and repeat the threat delivered at the robbery: "Give me all your money or I'll shoot." One man stepped out of line and yelled, "That's not what I said!"

YOU PUT YOUR LEFT FOOT IN, YOU TAKE YOUR LEFT FOOT OUT . . .

*U*sually escape plans are hatched by a team of prisoners who work in tandem to pull off their self-awarded release program. But one convict in the Henry County, Georgia, jail masterminded this prison escape on his own. Using a gun he had smuggled into his cell, he was able to get the drop on four guards. He ushered them into his cell and locked the door. Slowly creeping down the hall with the loaded weapon, he thought he was home free. But he'd overlooked the fact that all prison guards carry walkie-talkies, and that's what they used to inform the front-desk guards of an unwanted (or wanted) visitor. Having added attempted escape to his charges, our quickly caught con will be a visitor to the jail for a long time now.

NO DEPOSIT, NO RETURN

A man with a neat military haircut marched into the Fort
Belvoir Federal Credit Union and stood in line for the next
teller. One of the tellers thought she recognized the young man
and signaled him to come to her window. The man politely
asked the teller if she would wire $2,900 to his home in Texas
and also gave her a large pile of money to be deposited into his
account. "It couldn't be him," she must have thought to herself
as she went into the back room with the money. Acting on a
hunch, she decided to check the serial numbers on the top two
five-dollars bills. The bills matched those of the $4,759 that had
been taken in a robbery twelve days earlier. That's where she
had seen the young man before–standing in front of her nearly
two weeks ago, without a mask, robbing the bank. She called
the police. When the military police arrived, they were surprised
to find one of their own accused of robbing the bank and then
trying to deposit the money he'd stolen back into his account–a
man who, as a private in the military police, had undergone FBI
training on handling bank robberies. I guess he was trained in
the proper way of halting a bank robbery, not conducting one.

TAKEN FOR A RIDE

The man's eyes darted around the bank as he reached into his pocket and pulled out the crumpled holdup note. The teller at the Canadian Imperial Bank of Commerce in Gatineau, Quebec, accepted the note, unfolded it, but wasn't able to read it. The note was written in English, and the teller only understood French. She left the robber standing there and took the note to some other tellers for assistance. The man began to feel uneasy as a crowd gathered around the teller to help her translate the note. Panic got the best of him, and he dashed out of the bank into his getaway car—a taxi he had waiting around the corner. He gave the driver instructions to take him across the river to downtown Ottawa and sat back in the cab to calm his nerves. Once in the city, the man thought he would be able to go through with the robbery again and told the driver to turn the car around and head back to Gatineau. The driver looked at the haggard man sitting in the backseat and asked if he had enough money to pay the fare. Checking his pockets, the man admitted that he was short of cash and couldn't pay the meter. The driver slammed on the brakes, got out of his car, and called the police. The man was arrested and charged with armed robbery in connection with the failed attempt at the bank. He was later charged with a second count of armed robbery involving a Bank of Nova Scotia in Gatineau. Said Sergeant Richard Longpre of the Gatineau Police Department, "It wasn't such a smooth job by that guy."

TIMING IS EVERYTHING

*T*iming is of the utmost importance when one is attempting to rob a bank. Timing to hit the bank when it has the most money in its vaults, timing between the accomplices, and timing of the getaway are all crucial elements of a successful bank robbery. One of the most critical elements of time, however, is making sure the bank is open in the first place. "They just made mistakes in their times," said holdup squad detective Mike Earl. "Usually they plan a little better. But that's how we catch these guys . . . some of them are pretty stupid." Detective Earl was talking about an attempted bank robbery of the Bank of Nova Scotia in Toronto. Four men whose intention it was to rob the bank ran to the glass doors, grabbed the door handles, and pulled—nothing happened. The bank hadn't opened for business yet. The tellers inside were startled by the four men furiously pulling at the locked doors and quickly alerted the police. The men looked at their watches, looked at each other in disgust, jumped back into their black Honda, and left. They were, for all practical purposes, robbers ahead of their time.

THE SEVEN OOPS

*I*t was a yet-to-be-solved crime wave in Albany, Georgia: three bank robberies and three business robberies all attributed to seven criminal cohorts. An anonymous tip led the police to a residence that turned into a gold mine—all seven of the suspected robbers lived there. When confronted with the evidence the police had gathered against them and after a few short minutes of questioning, the seven confessed to the string of robberies. Even if they hadn't confessed to the crimes, they had already framed themselves—literally. One of the criminals was an amateur photographer and had taken photos of every robbery they had committed. The photographs were enlarged and proudly displayed on the walls for everyone to see—even the police. The next time they were in front of a camera was for their mug shots.

WHAT GOES UP MUST COME DOWN

*I*n police jargon, a criminal's MO means his modus operandi (method of operating)—basically, a pattern one routinely follows when conducting a crime. But in this case this criminal's MO should stand for "mostly obtuse." Here's the sequence of events that led to this man's fortunate (for him) capture. First, the thief cut his hand badly when he broke through the roof of a liquor store in San Antonio, Texas. He jumped down through the hole but soon realized that he didn't know how to hoist the stolen liquor up through the opening in the roof. He picked up a bottle of whiskey, took careful aim, and tossed the bottle toward the opening. The bottle missed the hole, smashed to the ground, and set off the burglar alarm. The burglar (I even hate to use that word) slipped on the spilled liquor, fell to the floor, and cut himself on the broken glass. As he was scrambling, empty-handed, back through the hole in the ceiling, his wallet fell out of his pocket and landed on the floor. Once on the roof, our thwarted thief took in a deep breath of fresh air, turned around, and fell off the roof. He limped away, battered, beaten, and bleeding, and left an easy-to-follow crimson trail of blood from the crime scene to his house—less than a block from the store.

NOT A GOOD HUMOR MAN

The police in Potomac, Maryland, in response to a call about a home burglary, were patrolling the area around the crime scene. They noticed a man sitting in a car and watched as he threw a Popsicle stick out of the window and onto the road, unwrapped another Popsicle, and put it in his mouth. Two officers got out of their patrol car and approached the man and soon had him under arrest. Was he arrested for littering? Nope. He was arrested for the burglary. The police knew they had the right man, as the only thing stolen during the robbery was a box of Popsicles.

A ROSE BY ANY OTHER NAME . . .

*T*he editorial page of a local newspaper offers an excellent opportunity for one to speak one's mind about
issues of concern. One such letter that appeared in the
Kingsport (Tennessee) Times-News was focused on exposing
conditions in local jails. Drafted by inmate Travis Nelms,
who had been incarcerated nine times in three years, the
letter read, in part, "We the inmates here at the Sullivan
County Jail [are] concerned that here we all [are] treated
as criminals." I guess you can't blame the guy for trying to
write a wrong.

YOU CAN'T WIN 'EM ALL

A man called 911 reporting that he had just been robbed of over $2,000 in cash. The police were dispatched, and they found the man beaten and bruised and very angry. It took the police only a few minutes to get there because they had just previously been summoned to respond to a bank robbery in the same exact area. The robbery victim quickly approached the patrol car and angrily explained to them what had happened. He admitted he was the man who'd robbed the bank. But the real crime, to his mind, was the fact that someone saw him rob the bank, jumped him, beat him up, and took the stolen money. The battered bank robber demanded that the police find the man who'd mugged him and gave them a very good description of the perpetrator. The mugger was never found, but the empty-handed (and empty-headed) bank robber was sentenced to a rather long stretch in the county pen.

GETTING A LEG UP ON CRIME

A man who robbed a St. Louis grocery store, to avoid being identified, had made sure he was carrying a spare shirt in his back pocket. In the process of changing on the run, however, the robber forgot that he had also placed his gun in the same pocket.

When he reached for the shirt, he hit the trigger of the gun and shot himself in the leg. It wasn't long before the police found the bleeding robber in the backseat of a car just two blocks from the grocery store, passed out from the excruciating pain. He was placed in custody and rushed to the hospital. He survived his injury and was later convicted of the robbery. During his getaway, the guy had probably thought he was a fast runner–but not faster than a speeding bullet.